RY JOBS

PARATROOPERS

What It Takes to Join the Elite

TIM RIPLEY

Cavendish
Square

New York

Published in 2016 by Cavendish Square Publishing, LLC
243 5th Avenue, Suite 136, New York, NY 10016

© 2016 Brown Bear Books Ltd

First Edition

Website: cavendishsq.com

CPSIA Compliance Information: Batch #WS15CSQ

Library of Congress Cataloging-in-Publication Data

Ripley, Tim.
 Paratroopers : what it takes to join the elite / Tim Ripley.
    pages cm. — (Military jobs)
 Includes bibliographical references and index.
 ISBN 978-1-50260-516-0 (hardcover) ISBN 978-1-50260-517-7 (ebook)
 1. United States. Army—Parachute troops. 2. United States. Army—Parachute troops—Vocational guidance. 3. Airborne operations (Military science) I. Title.

 UD483.R55 2015
 356'.16602373—dc23

                      2015002267

For Brown Bear Books Ltd:
Editorial Director: Lindsey Lowe
Managing Editor: Tim Cooke
Children's Publisher: Anne O'Daly
Design Manager: Keith Davis
Designer: Lynne Lennon
Picture Manager: Sophie Mortimer

Picture Credits:
T=Top, C=Center, B=Bottom, L=Left, R=Right

Front Cover: U.S. Department of Defense
All images U.S. Department of Defense except: Air and Space Museum: 7; Robert Hunt Library: 6.
Artistic Effects: Shutterstock

Brown Bear Books has made every attempt to contact the copyright holder.
If you have any information please contact licensing@brownbearbooks.co.uk

We believe the extracts included in this book to be material in the public domain.
Anyone having any further information should contact licensing@brownbearbooks.co.uk.

Manufactured in the United States of America

CONTENTS

INTRODUCTION

It takes a special kind of soldier to jump out of an airplane, float silently to the ground—often in darkness—and be ready to fight in moments. The paratroopers of the US Army have what it takes.

Because they are easy to transport, paratroopers are usually among the first soldiers on the ground in any conflict. They only jump with what they can carry, and because of that, they are trained to fight in small groups and to use their own initiative.

Most paratroopers in the US Army belong to the two airborne divisions, the 82nd "All-American" Division and the 101st "Screaming Eagles" Division. They are infantry soldiers who have trained to parachute into battle or to be landed on the battlefield by helicopters in air assaults. Many other units also have airborne elements who are trained paratroopers. Parachuting is also a basic skill of the various special forces, including the Army Rangers, the Green Berets, and the Navy SEALs. They parachute in to begin a mission without being detected.

 A paratrooper uses cords attached to his parachute canopy to steer toward a landing zone during a mass drop.

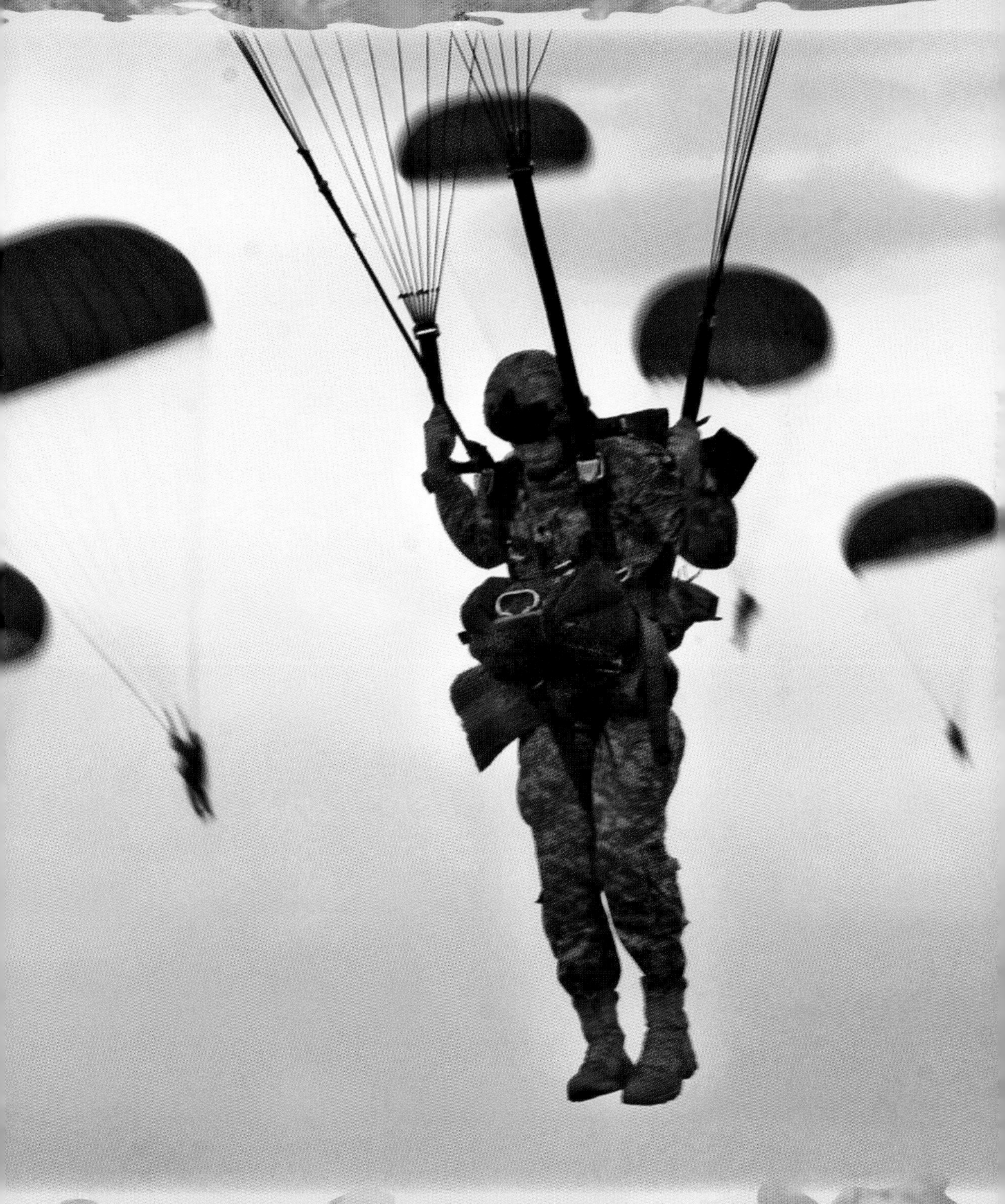

HISTORY

The US Army realized the benefits of using paratroopers early in World War II (1939–1945). America's first paratroopers went into action in August 1942 as part of the invasion of Nazi-occupied North Africa.

Within a year, the US Army had formed the 82nd Airborne Division. In July 1943, its paratroopers spearheaded Allied landings on Sicily. By the time Allied forces invaded Normandy on D-Day in 1944, the US Army had four divisions of paratroopers. The 82nd "All-American" Division and the 101st "Screaming Eagles" Division served with distinction in Normandy and in Holland during the advance on Arnhem. The campaigns cemented the place of paratroopers in US military history.

After World War II
Since World War II, US paratroopers have jumped into action in military campaigns all

US paratroopers prepare to leave their airplane over Normandy, France, during the Allied invasion of France on D-Day, June 6, 1944.

around the world. They fought in Korea in the 1950s, Vietnam in the 1960s, Grenada in the 1980s, and Iraq and Afghanistan since 2000. They have a reputation as elite units among the US military.

Emergency Response

The US Army maintains strong forces of paratroopers on alert. They are the 911 emergency force in time of crisis because they can get to any trouble spot quicker than other troops. These rapid-reaction forces are ready to intervene anywhere at short notice.

 C-119 transport planes drop "sticks" of US paratroopers over Korea in November 1952.

EYEWITNESS

"American parachutists—devils in baggy pants—are less than one hundred yards from my outpost. I can't sleep at night; they pop up from nowhere and we never know when or how they will strike next. Seems like the black-hearted devils are everywhere."

—Diary of a dead German officer, Anzio, 1944

WHAT IT TAKES

All airborne forces share the unique experience of parachuting into enemy territory. America's paratroopers wear the red beret with pride. It is the headgear of airborne forces around the world.

The same spirit that motivated US paratroopers in World War II still motivates today's airborne warriors. Paratroopers need nerves of steel to jump out of an aircraft 500 feet (152 meters) above the ground, which is too low for a reserve parachute to work. They might have to jump

A member of the 82nd Airborne drops onto pads from a net on an assault course.

at night and in the face of enemy fire. Once on the ground, they have to be able to fight wherever they land, often without waiting for orders from their commanders.

Unique Character

Potential airborne warriors have to show they have the "right stuff" to be a paratrooper. Independence of spirit makes paratroopers stand out from soldiers who are more used to working to detailed orders. An ability to adapt, improvise, and overcome is at the heart of what makes paratroopers tick.

 Members of the 82nd Airborne Division wear their red berets during a ceremony marking a change of command.

IN ACTION

Women in the US Army can qualify from jump school, gain a paratrooper's wings, and wear the maroon beret. They are not allowed to become combat paratroopers but serve in noncombat roles. In April 2007, Monica Brown, a medical specialist with the 82nd Airborne, won the Silver Star for treating colleagues while under fire in Afghanistan.

⟩⟩ AIRBORNE SCHOOL

Potential paratroopers must join the US Army and complete basic training before they can volunteer for airborne school at Fort Benning, Georgia. If they are successful, they can apply to join an airborne unit.

The three-week-long basic airborne course is split into phases. Students first have to learn how to land safely. They practice landing positions and drills to avoid unnecessary injury. They are also taught how to put on their parachute harness and how to open a parachute.

Simulated Jumps

In the second week, students make simulated jumps and landings from a tall tower. Students' parachutes automatically deploy, so they

⟩⟩ A paratrooper has his jumping position adjusted by a colleague during training.

are free to concentrate on their landings. These jumps are a chance for students to learn how to identify and solve problems with their parachutes.

Recruits practice landing falls. They roll to absorb the impact of hitting the ground.

Jumping from Planes

In the last week of the course, students make five jumps from aircraft. On each successive jump, students carry a heavier load. On the final jump, they carry full combat gear and weapons. Students who successfully complete the course are awarded the celebrated airborne wings and can wear the red beret. They are now fully fledged paratroopers.

EYEWITNESS

"It takes courage to jump from an airplane while in flight, wearing equipment strapped to your legs, and sometimes at night. But after completing five jumps, you earn your silver wings. You become a sky soldier. You become AIRBORNE!"

—Daniel Brankin, US Army paratrooper

⟫ UNIT JUMP TRAINING

A new paratrooper joins the airborne divisions or an airborne brigade assigned to another unit. Training is not over, however. Paratroopers still have to learn a whole range of skills.

Paratroopers of the 82nd Airborne Division descend after a mass jump from a C-17 Globemaster airplane.

One of the most potentially dangerous skills to learn is jumping as part of a large group of paratroopers. Airborne units might be asked to jump in large

formations from multiple aircraft. They have to avoid hitting any colleagues in the air, while remaining close enough to each other to land together.

 Paratroopers from the 82nd Airborne Division practice assembling into a "stack" ready to clear a building while covering each other.

On the Ground

Once paratroopers hit the ground, they are trained on how to avoid being hit by later waves of men or cargo pallets. They collect their equipment and muster near the drop zone. This has to be done quickly to make the most of the element of surprise so they can secure their objectives.

IN ACTION

Mass parachute drops involve not only waves of paratroopers but also dropping cargo pallets containing vehicles, howitzers, supplies, and ammunuition. Training for these large drops is long and demanding. Paratroopers learn how to pack cargo pallets and then load them onto aircraft.

⟫ AIR ASSAULT TRAINING

Since the Vietnam War in the 1960s, US airborne units have been capable of being delivered to the battlefield by helicopter rather than by parachute.

Paratroopers pull guard duty as the Black Hawk helicopter that has just put them on the ground takes off again.

The Army calls these helicopter operations "air assault" missions. The troops who carry them out have special training in what to do if a helicopter crashes.

On the Ground

In addition to basic safety skills, air assault troopers learn how to rapidly exit helicopters. Often a helicopter can land them directly on the ground. If no safe landing zone is available, however, the paratroopers drop by rope from a hovering helicopter. Hovering or stationary helicopters are vulnerable to enemy ground fire, so any exit has to be made at speed. Isolated airborne detachments depend on resupply by transport helicopters. Paratroopers learn to safely unhook cargo loads carried beneath helicopters in slings.

 Men from the 1st Combat Brigade of the 82nd Airborne prepare to hook a 1055mm howitzer to a Black Hawk helicopter.

EYEWITNESS

"The Air Assault course is only ten days long, but it is a rigorous ten days. You must be able to focus and study while completing tasks including an obstacle course and confidence course, ruck marches, and physical training sessions."

—**Matthew Ives, cadet, Airborne School**

LASER-COMBAT SIMULATION

As in other parts of the US Army, airborne combat training uses a Multiple Integrated Laser Engagement Simulation (MILES) system.

US paratroopers on a base in Iraq practice an assault using night vision goggles and laser weapons.

Every soldier taking part in combat training drills has a laser attachment on his weapon. It "shoots" beams of light at a target. Each soldier also wears a vest that contains laser detectors. If the soldier is "hit" by a laser beam, an alarm sounds. The soldier has to lie down to switch the alarm off.

Realistic Training

MILES equipment has changed how US airborne units train for war. It allows soldiers to practice both their marksmanship and their ability to stay under cover. They can perfect these skills in a wide variety of situations. MILES devices can be fit to vehicles, helicopters, and other hardware, so battles involving every type of modern weapon can easily be simulated.

Airborne units being deployed overseas attend mission-rehearsal exercises at the Fort Polk Joint Readiness Training Center in Louisiana. The exercises are monitored by computers so that experts can review the soldiers' progress and help them improve.

A paratrooper from the 82nd Airborne uses a MILES weapon during a training exercise.

IN ACTION

In action in Iraq after the invasion of 2003, paratroopers of the 82nd Airborne used laser target designators to aim their weapons. A green laser beam points to where a bullet would strike. Iraqi civilians learned to recognize the beam as a warning that they were entering a dangerous area. That was enough to warn them to leave.

⮞⮞ EMERGENCY DEPLOYMENT READINESS

The 82nd Airborne Division is at the forefront of America's emergency reaction forces. Its mission is to be ready to deploy paratroopers anywhere in the world, 24/7, within eighteen hours' notice.

One of the Division's brigade combat teams is always on standby for what is termed emergency deployment readiness. The brigade has to be able to fly anywhere in the world. Its primary mission would mostly be to seize an airfield. This is essential if follow-on forces are to be flown in by airplane. Depending on the size of the operation, all five thousand of the brigade's paratroopers must be ready to go into action at the same time, along with all their equipment.

⮞⮞ **Special Forces paratroopers prepare for a training jump from a helicopter.**

Against the Clock

To keep the 82nd Airborne on its toes, its "ready" brigade is put through timed drills without warning. The command team recalls the troops to barracks without telling them if the recall is a drill or for real. The troops rush to break out weapons, ammunition, and other equipment. Pre-loaded cargo pallets of ammunition, food, water, and fuel are readied for loading onto transport aircraft. Exercise controllers use stopwatches to monitor all aspects of the mobilization to check the speed of the brigade's reaction.

 A paratrooper pulls security as his colleagues clear a building during an exercise.

EYEWITNESS

"Here in the 82nd Airborne Division, everyone in the division has a mind-set and a sense of preparedness to jump, fight, and win tonight. To maintain that and all the systems that allow us to do it, we have to exercise it."

—**Colonel Brian Winski, 82nd Airborne, 2014**

▶▶ STRATEGIC STRIKE MISSIONS

Only the US military can send an airborne brigade anywhere in the world at a moment's notice. This strategic capability is used on the orders of the President of the United States alone.

Strike missions are only launched when the US national command authority wants to turn world events in America's favor. Such missions have to achieve a specific strategic goal.

The highest strategic priority of US airborne forces is to gain an entry point into a theater of operations. The paratroopers must capture an airfield and then defend it from counterattack while reinforcements are flown in. Setting up a bridgehead in hostile territory also requires supporting elements such as combat air controllers, airfield operations experts, and bomb disposal teams.

Paratroopers from the 82nd Airborne wait to jump from a C-17 Globemaster aircraft.

Strategic Advantage

US airborne forces might also be ordered to seize the strategic assets of an enemy country or terrorist group. The target could be a nation's nuclear weapons sites or government buildings. These missions are planned to achieve their objectives with one swift, decisive action.

The possession of powerful airborne forces gives US commanders a strategic advantage. It also has a psychological effect on enemies. The US government sometimes states publicly that the 82nd Airborne are ready to act. Such a declaration is made to intimidate opponents in times of crisis.

Light infantry prepare to engage the enemy in the Chaki Wardak region of Afghanistan.

IN ACTION

Military planners undertake both tactical and strategic missions. A tactical mission aims for an immediate victory. A strategic mission is part of a long-term campaign to weaken the enemy.

▶▶ TACTICAL INSERTIONS

Parachute assaults can make a decisive impact in battle. US commanders can send airborne troops in to a whole range of different combat situations.

One reason to use paratroopers is their ability to land silently or at night, anywhere on the battlefield. Paratroopers dropped from fast-flying aircraft give enemy troops no chance to organize their defenses. Paratroopers drop around their positions and overwhelm the defenders.

 Paratroopers from the 173rd Airborne Brigade take up a defensive position.

A paratrooper from the 1st Brigade Combat Team of the 82nd Airborne jumps from a helicopter.

A night assault is a classic use of airborne forces. It requires US paratroopers to be aggressive and to use their own initiative to take the fight to the enemy. It often results in violent gunfights as paratroopers assault the very heart of enemy positions.

Effective Weapons

The fact that paratroopers can be put in place without being noticed makes them highly effective. They can encircle enemy troops, sometimes working with troops on the ground. The enemy might not realize they are surrounded until it is too late.

Even the the threat of parachute drops can gain US forces an advantage. If enemy commanders just don't known where they will be attacked next, they have to spread their forces out, making them less able to resist a specific attack.

EYEWITNESS

"Each one of these paratroopers is the equivalent of ten to fifteen normal humans."

—Colonel William C. Mayville, 173rd Division, Iraq, 2003

AIR ASSAULT

If paratroopers capture an airfield, waves of giant C-17 cargo aircraft can deliver dozens of helicopters for air assaults. The AH-64 Apache and UH-60 Black Hawk helicopters can be rapidly reassembled. They can then be used to expand the area under US control.

Paratroopers run to set up a defensive perimeter after leaving a US Marines CH-53 Sea King helicopter.

Once helicopters are operational, they begin ferrying US paratroopers on air assault operations. These operations begin with Apache attack helicopters laying down intense suppressive fire around the landing zones. This temporarily pins down enemy

 Airborne soldiers ride in a Chinook helicopter on their way to make an air assault in Afghanistan in 2008.

troops. With the enemy taking cover, waves of Black Hawks carrying assault troops can fly in.

Securing a Position

The Apaches remain above the landing zones while the Black Hawks drop off the assault force in case the enemy tries to attack the transport helicopters as they land. Once on the ground, assault troops move to secure a defensive perimeter around the airfield or landing zone to create a base for future operations. Behind the air assault troops, more helicopters bring in additional ammunition and supplies. Other helicopters carry mortars and artillery to provide ground-based fire support.

EYEWITNESS

"I saw the ground for the first time from that altitude. But it was so far away, it looked surreal, not dangerous. It looked like a picture."

—John T. Reed, US author

COUNTERINSURGENCY
OPERATIONS

US airborne units are some of the country's most highly trained light infantry. They are often the first units called upon to take on enemy insurgents.

 US paratroopers and Afghan police search a car in Khyar-Khot in 2010.

Counterinsurgency operations often take the form of small-scale battles. These often take place in built-up areas where there are large numbers of noncombatant civilians. Both sides compete to win the loyalty of the local population.

Small Forces

US airborne troops are specialists in this type of warfare. They can operate in small groups in isolated locations with limited fire support or armored vehicles. Small detachments of paratroopers operating among local populations can have a huge impact on events. They can break down into small patrols that move easily around villages or the back alleys of towns.

By moving among local people, paratroopers pick up invaluable intelligence about insurgent groups. This intelligence is used to plan offensive missions to defeat the insurgents in their hiding places. The next step for US forces is to set up small bases in villages and city districts. This reassures the population that they will be protected if they decide to support US forces in their efforts against the insurgents.

 A paratrooper from the 82nd Airborne Division searches a suspected insurgent compound in Ghazni province, Afghanistan.

IN ACTION

The key to sucessful counterinsurgency operations is intelligence. US forces gather information from local people. Paratroopers work closely with their colleagues from the Special Forces, who usually speak local languages. This helps them make allies in a community.

HUMANITARIAN AID MISSIONS

Earthquakes, hurricanes, and other natural disasters cause massive human suffering. US airborne forces are often the first on the scene to lead rescue efforts in dangerous and devastated areas.

 A soldier carries emergency meals for distribution after an earthquake in Haiti in 2010.

Paratroopers lead aid missions because they can get anywhere quickly in response to an emergency. Airborne units can move into action in a matter of hours.

On the Ground

The paratroopers take equipment to get damaged airfields back into action. This ensures that cargo planes can bring emergency supplies and personnel into the disaster zone. Airborne troops can also help search for survivors in collapsed buildings and help to build refugee camps. They collect corpses to prevent the spread of disease, or evacuate refugees to safety. The airborne spirit of "adapt, improvise, and overcome" is an essential part of success in such situations.

A colonel from the 101st Airborne Division hands out school supplies to girls in Nangarhar province, Afghanistan, in 2013.

EYEWITNESS

"We provide capabilities that no one else in the world can provide ... Our presence provides confidence that something can and will be done and we're exactly the right unit to accomplish this task."

—Maj. Gen. Garry Volesky, 101st Airborne, Liberia, during the Ebola crisis, 2014

SMALL ARMS

US paratroopers have to be self-sufficient in firepower. They land with the small arms they need to be able to fight until reinforcements and heavy weapons can reach them on the battlefield.

The primary rifle of US paratroopers is the Colt M4. This assault rifle can provide heavy suppressive fire if needed. The M4 often has an M203 grenade launcher attached beneath its barrel. This can lob a high-explosive grenade up to 1,300 feet (400 m).

 This paratrooper's M4 rifle has a laser target designator fitted beneath the barrel.

 A team from the 82nd Airborne Division fires an FGM-148 Javelin missile in Iraq in 2008.

Heavy Weapons

To give paratrooper squads heavy fire, they use the M249 Squad Automatic Weapon or SAW. This can fire more than 800 rounds a minute at targets up to 1.8 miles (2,900 m) away.

As a last line of defense, all paratroopers carry a Beretta M9 pistol. If they are separated from their other weapons, the pistol gives them enough firepower to get out of dangerous situations.

COLT M4 ASSAULT RIFLE
Effective range: 656 yards (600 m) (2,410 km/h)
Caliber: .223 inches (5.66 mm)
Length: 29.75 inches (756 mm)
Weight: 7.5 pounds (3.4 kg)

IN ACTION

Paratroopers bring their own antitank firepower into combat with the FGM-148 missile. This laser-guided missile is programmed to strike the upper armor of enemy tanks. It has a range of 2.9 miles (4,750 m), meaning paratroopers can keep enemy armor at a safe distance.

▶▶ PARACHUTES AND DROP PALLETS

A paratrooper's life depends on his parachute. The T-11 parachute has proved itself reliable in combat. It is also steerable, so soldiers can all arrive safely in the landing zone at the same time.

The parachute can be used from as low as 550 feet (167 m). After leaving the aircraft, paratroopers are on the ground in about twenty-one seconds. This reduces the time they are vulnerable to enemy fire. The T-11 parachute can support up to

The parachute begins to open as a Jeep strapped to a cargo pallet is pushed from the rear of an aircraft.

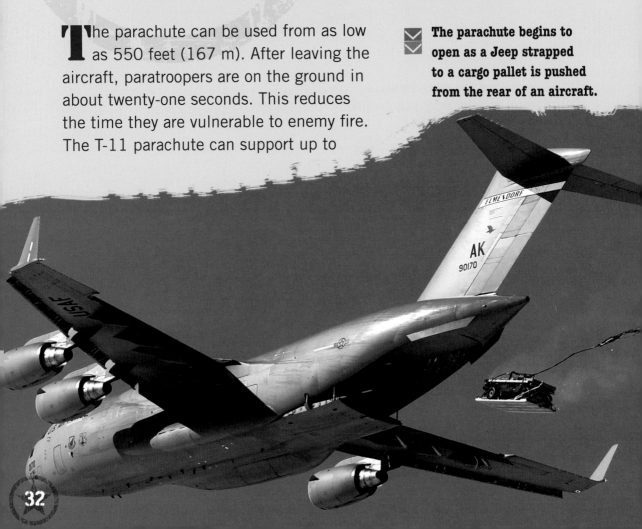

400 pounds (181 kg) of gear. The gear hangs on a line below the paratrooper during the jump.

Paratroopers steer their parachutes toward the landing zone during a mass drop exercise.

Supply Drops

On the ground, paratroopers need vehicles, artillery, and supplies. These are dropped on pallets rigged with parachutes. Cargo pallets are guided by the Joint Precision Airdrop System (JPADS). It uses a guidance, navigation, and control system to fly the pallet to the drop zone. Its gliding ram-air parachute gets it within 165–245 feet (50–75 m) of the target.

IN ACTION

Ram-air parachutes are usually shaped a little like rectangular mattresses. They have two layers of fabric. A system of vents at the front of the parachute fills the cells between the layers with high-pressure air. Ram-air parachutes can glide farther than normal parachutes, and are easier to steer.

C-130 AND C-17 AIRLIFTERS

The job of delivering paratroopers to the battlefield belongs to the US Air Force. It uses its giant transport airplanes, called airlifters.

For fifty years, US paratroopers have jumped from the Lockheed C-130 Hercules. The Hercules can carry sixty-four fully equipped paratroopers and drop them from as low as 550 feet (167 m). The aircraft is designed for static-line parachuting, which is when the parachute opens as the jumper leaves the airplane. Paratroopers can jump from the side doors or rear ramp. Because of the noise, the aircraft has red and green "jump lights" inside. They tell the paratroopers when to move into position and when to jump.

 Paratroopers leave a C-17 Globemaster during a static-line jump.

 Paratroopers wait to board a fleet of C-130 Hercules airlifters ready for a mass jump.

The rugged Hercules can also be rigged to carry up to six pallets of cargo, weighing up to 20 tons (18 tonnes), or two HUMVEE armored trucks that can be loaded up its rear cargo ramp.

C-17 Globemaster

For strategic operations, the US Air Force uses its Boeing C-17 Globemaster III airlifters. These giant transports have a range of 5,000 miles (8,047 km). If they are refueled in the air, the range is several times that distance.

The airlifter is an effective strategic weapon anywhere in the world. The C-17 can carry one hundred paratroopers or up to eighteen cargo pallets.

EYEWITNESS

"If you've never ridden on a C-130 think darkness and noise. There is a series of round portholes along each side, so you get a line of round spotlights piercing the darkness, but that only heightens the effect of the dark."

—Stephen H. King, Airborne School

 HELICOPTERS

The US Army's combat helicopters give America's paratroopers a huge battlefield advantage. The Black Hawk delivers them into combat, while the Apache gunship protects them from the air.

The two-crew Boeing AH-64D Apache attack helicopter has awesome firepower. It also has powerful night vision sensors to allow it to detect enemy troops. At the heart of the Apache's weapon system is its AGM-114 Hellfire missiles and its 30 mm

 The Apache gunship is heavily armed. It can hover above landing zones to protect paratroopers as they land by helicopter.

automatic cannon. The cannon beneath the helicopter's nose is "slaved" to the pilot's helmet. When the pilot looks at a target, the gun automatically points in the same direction so targets can be engaged in a fraction of a second.

 An air assault team is briefed before climbing into a UH-60 Black Hawk for a mission.

UH-60 Black Hawk

Carrying US paratroopers into action is the mission of the Sikorsky UH-60 Black Hawk helicopter. It has been in frontline service with the US Army since 1978. The Black Hawk can carry a squad of eleven paratroopers inside or 9,000 pounds (4,082 kg) of cargo in a sling beneath the helicopter. It is one of the fastest troop transport helicopters. It can swoop above the battlefield at up to 183 miles per hour (294 kmh).

EYEWITNESS

"Most of [the Army] has to air land. They can't jump in a Bradley or a tank company or a Stryker company."

—**Brian Winski, Deputy Commander, 82nd Airborne Division**

OPERATION DESERT SHIELD, 1990

On August 2, 1990, Iraq invaded its tiny neighbor, Kuwait. US President George H. W. Bush worried that Saddam Hussein would next send his troops into Saudi Arabia to seize the Gulf kingdom's oil fields.

 US paratroopers patrol in Saudi Arabia wearing gas masks in case of an attack with chemical weapons.

Only a week after the invasion, the 82nd Airborne Division's ready brigade landed at Saudi Arabia's Dhahran airbase. The paratroopers provided security as US Air Force F-15 Eagle fighters arrived to boost air defenses.

 US paratroopers arrive at Dhahran Airbase in Saudi Arabia.

They took chemical defense suits and decontamination equipment in case Iraq used chemical weapons.

In the Desert

The rest of the 82nd Airborne soon arrived. Within days, the division was ready to move out into the desert to set up defensive positions. The division lacked heavy armor and artillery. Some paratroopers joked they were just "speed bumps" in the desert for Saddam Hussein's tanks. The deployment had the desired effect,

however. The Iraqi president stopped his tanks at the Saudi border and missed his chance to take over 40 percent of the world's oil reserves.

EYEWITNESS

"I can only remember thinking, after years of training and preparing ... I'm ready to die for my country if need be. But I'm not prepared to let one of my brothers die. I was nervous for their safety."

—Les Calton, 82nd Airborne, Operation Desert Shield

▶▶ IRAQ, 2003

During planning for the 2003 invasion of Iraq, US commanders hoped to open a northern front from Turkey. Days before US troops were scheduled to land, Turkey closed its borders to the Americans.

⌄ **Smoke billows from a building during a 101st Airborne attack in Mosul in 2003. Two of Saddam Hussein's sons died during the assault.**

A nother way had to be found to get US troops into northern Iraq, where Kurdish fighters were exposed to Saddam Hussein's troops. The answer was the US European Command's reserve airborne task force, the 173rd Airborne Brigade. On March 26, 2003, 954 paratroopers jumped over Bashur Airfield in Iraq.

Airfield Secured

The jump took a total of fifty-eight seconds, but the landing force was strung out over a 10,000-yard (9.1-km) drop zone. It took fifteen hours before it was completely assembled. The paratroopers secured the airfield, allowing C-17s to land and bring in heavy armor. Over the next ninety-six hours, more C-17s landed the remaining 1,200 soldiers of the 173rd Brigade, as well as their vehicles. By March 29, the entire brigade was in Iraq. They were ready to conduct offensive operations.

 Soldiers of the 101st Airborne Division fire a missile at a target in Mosul, Iraq, in 2003.

EYEWITNESS

"The lights of a Kurdish village were visible below. 'One minute!' yelled the jumpmasters. Some men were throwing up. Others were on their knees, sagging under the weight of their gear. The largest combat parachute assault since World War II was under way."

—Ken Dilanian, *Philadelphia Inquirer*, Bashur, March 2003

▶▶ NEW ORLEANS, 2005

In August 2005, Hurricane Katrina struck New Orleans in Louisiana. As the flood defenses broke, much of the city was submerged underwater.

Thousands of residents fled the city. Others were trapped in their homes or sought shelter in the Superdome stadium. Some 1,800 civilians were killed in the disaster. They came mainly from the

 Men from the 82nd Airborne use a rubber boat to look for people trapped in their homes.

 After the floodwaters receded, airborne soldiers patrolled downtown New Orleans. Such patrols helped keep order and prevent looting.

poorer parts of the city. Following criticism of government inactivity, President George W. Bush sent military forces to New Orleans.

Saving Lives

The 82nd Airborne Division was on the ground within seven hours of getting their orders. Helicopters arrived at New Orleans airport and soon airborne artillerymen were working to clear runways. Within twelve hours, thousands of civilian evacuees were flown out of the disaster area on military transport aircraft. The division's medical unit set up a hospital in the city and communications specialists set up a radio network to assist aid workers. Paratroopers arrived at the Superdome to begin the evacuation of the thousands of refugees who had nowhere else to go.

EYEWITNESS

"When you tell the 82nd Airborne, 'Secure New Orleans,' they come in and they know exactly what to do and it gets done."

—Bill Leighty, governor's staff, Virginia

>>> COUNTERINSURGENCY IN IRAQ

After Saddam Hussein's government collapsed in April 2003, the US military occupied Iraq. It had to move quickly to try to restore government, law and order, and essential services to the country.

Paratroopers watch their helicopter leaving after dropping them for a patrol in Iraq in 2005.

The 82nd Airborne's 2nd Brigade secured a region around the cities of Fallujah and Ramadi. Its troops were in Fallujah when a protest became a gun battle that left several civilians dead. The event marked the start of the Iraqi insurgency.

A Year of Fighting

Over the next year, the US paratroopers found themselves under repeated attack in Fallujah as the insurgents recruited more and more fighters. The airborne troops tried to win the support of

A paratrooper squeezes through a doorway while searching a compound for insurgents.

the local population by conducting "hearts and minds" aid missions. At the same time, they launched nighttime raids on the homes of suspected insurgents. They also set up regular road blocks to try to prevent insurgent movements.

The 2003 deployment of the 2nd Brigade was the first of five brigade-sized deployments to Iraq by paratroopers of the 82nd Airborne Division. They fought insurgents across the country.

EYEWITNESS

"The Iraqis rely on you and trust you to take care of them. And knowing you can help was an amazing feeling. We treated lot of small children with malaria, a lot of burn injuries and bullet wounds."

—Dustin Lehmann,
US Army medic,
Habbaniyah, Iraq, 2005

45

GLOSSARY

air assault A mission in which soldiers go into action by helicopter.

armor Heavily protected vehicles such as tanks.

canopy The fabric part of a parachute that expands as it fills with air.

change of command A ceremony marking a handover of power from one military unit to another.

compound A building or group of buildings that is enclosed by a wall.

counterinsurgency A campaign that tries to defeat insurgents by removing their support.

covert Describes something done in secret.

deployment Moving military forces into position for action.

evacuee Someone who is moved away from a place of danger.

howitzer An artillery weapon with a short barrel for firing missiles in a high arc.

humanitarian Describes something done to improve the welfare of other people for no personal gain.

insurgents Rebels fighting against a government or an invasion force.

intelligence Information about the enemy that has military value.

landing zone The place where a group of paratroopers intends to land together.

light infantry A type of soldier who goes into action without heavy equipment such as artillery.

looting The stealing of goods during a period of unrest.

muster To assemble troops in preparation for battle.

noncombatant Someone who is not engaged in fighting during a war, such as a civilian.

palette A flat, movable platform used to transport cargo.

paratrooper A soldier who parachutes into action.

stack A military formation in which a unit forms a thin line.

static-line jump A parachute jump in which parachutes are opened by cords as jumpers leave an airplane.

strategic Describes something that is related to overall victory in a war rather than victory in a battle.

tactical Describes something related to an immediate victory in a battle.

FURTHER INFORMATION

BOOKS

Cooke, Tim. *U.S. Airborne Forces*. Ultimate Special Forces. New York: PowerKids Press, 2012.

David, Jack. *Air Force Air Commandos*. Torque: Armed Forces. Minneapolis, MN: Bellwether Media, 2009.

Kennedy, Robert C. *Life as a Paratrooper*. High Interest Books: On Duty. New York: Children's Press, 2000.

McGowen, Tim. *Assault from the Sky: Airborne Infantry of World War II*. Military Might. Minneapolis, MN: 21st Century Books, 2002.

Montana, Jack. *Parachute Regiment*. Special Forces: Protecting, Building, Teaching, and Fighting. Broomall, PA: Mason Crest, 2011.

Nardo, Don. *Special Operations: Paratroopers*. Military Experience. Greensboro, NC: Morgan Reynolds Publishing, 2012.

WEBSITES

www.goarmy.com/soldier-life/being-a-soldier/ongoing-training/specialized-schools/airborne-school.html
US Army page on the experience of going to Airborne School.

www.military.com/military-fitness/army-special-operations/army-airborne-pft
Details of the Personal Fitness Test for the airborne divisions and how to prepare for it.

www.ww2-airborne.us/18corps/101abn/101_overview.html
The story of the 101st Airborne Division in World War II.

Publisher's note to educators and parents: Our editors have carefully reviewed these websites to ensure that they are suitable for students. Many websites change frequently, however, and we cannot guarantee that a site's future contents will continue to meet our high standards of quality and educational value. Be advised that students should be closely supervised whenever they access the Internet.

INDEX